QUIET TIMES

with

ANDREW MURRAY

A Life Essentials Journal

QUIET TIMES
with
ANDREW
MURRAY

COMPILED AND INTRODUCED
BY JAMES S. BELL, JR.

MOODY PRESS
CHICAGO

All Scripture quotations, unless otherwise indicated, are taken from the New King James Version. Copyright © 1979, 1980, 1982 by Thomas Nelson, Inc. Used by permission. All rights reserved.

Scripture quotations marked KJV are taken from the King James Version.

Library of Congress Cataloging-in-Publication Data

Murray, Andrew, 1828–1917.
  Quiet times with Andrew Murray / compiled and introduced by James S. Bell, Jr.
    p. cm.
  ISBN ISBN 0-8024-7047-5
  1. Meditations. I. Bell, James S. II. Title
BV4832.2 .M89 2000
242--dc21

00-056113

1 3 5 7 9 10 8 6 4 2

Printed in the United States of America

*To the
Baker, Lewis, Dennis, and Thurmond families,
who have been a source of encouragement
to me over the years.*

CONTENTS

INTRODUCTION

$\mathcal{E}$ach year hundreds of brand-new Christian books appear not only in Christian bookstores but, increasingly, in secular bookstores and even in retail chain stores throughout the country. It is exciting to see so many topics addressed from a Christian point of view, reaching such a large potential audience with a message of hope and truth.

Though it is important to be relevant and contemporary, this trend may also tend to obscure the fact that there is a huge wealth of Christian classics written over a century ago which are available to help us grow in areas far more important—in the essentials of our relationship with God.

The latest publishing trends may address issues rarely touched upon in the past: taking care of your physical health, raising your teenager, or even the ethics of genetic engineering. But the basics of our relationship with God never change, and it is here, in our response to His love and commandments, where our greatest needs lie, whether they are felt or not.

Our greatest challenges lie in understanding the teachings found in His Word, obeying them, and bearing fruit consistent with the nature and purposes of Christ. It is in these areas that classic Christian works excel. At times we may find that the essentials of the faith get pushed to the periphery in our Christian reading and may be covered superficially even in our devotional life.

One advantage the classics retain in books related to the "Christian living" or "spiritual growth" categories is that they have withstood the scrutiny of succeeding generations. The fruit of the ministries of such great preachers as D.L. Moody, Andrew Murray, and Charles Spurgeon included the conversion of countless thousands of souls as well as strengthening the maturity and impact of the church here and abroad.

The numerous volumes of Moody, Spurgeon, and Murray have sold millions of copies in numerous editions, and most titles remain on bookstore shelves today. Perhaps one reason for this was that their main target was not the educated elite but the masses. They geared the message of the Gospel to be understood by the average working-class person of the time and thus their style, by and large, is not archaic today.

I do not mean to imply that they shied away from in-depth biblical knowledge, but rather that they communicated in a simple and straightforward manner as men who truly "knew their Bibles" and had a passion for the average Christian to grow to his or her full stature in Christ.

The preaching and the writings that follow in this "Quiet Times" series are designed to shake you out of your spiritual lethargy and challenge you to live a life of deeply committed discipleship. They continually focus on the great love of God in Christ and yet specify the need to be like Him and separate from the world. This series is not for complacent Christians who want to merely feel better and enhance the quality of their private lives, but those who want to embark upon the exciting adventure of surrendering all to God. Staying with the essentials, their topics include abiding in Christ, servanthood, prayer, the meaning of the Gospel, the character of God, repentance, and other central teachings and practices at the heart of our walk with God.

Perhaps what makes this series most distinctive is its format. These three great preachers promoted the spiritual disciplines in their ministries, and they wholeheartedly supported biblical meditation and prayer, as well as the application of biblical principles—all of which are found in this journal format.

With the introduction of the LifeEssentials journals that comprise the Quiet Times series, I have attempted to bring together two means of getting closer to God. Most journals today consist of blank pages where we articulate our deepest prayers and monitor our spiritual progress. Yet there is no immediate inspiring text to respond to and record our understanding.

At the same time solid Christian books of the Moody-Murray-Spurgeon variety allow no room for devotional activity: the ability to write prayers, express our understanding of key elements of the text, and make commitments to these same principles. The LifeEssentials journals combine text, prayers, questions, and goals in order to offer the reader a high-quality and satisfying devotional experience.

This book, *Quiet Times with Andrew Murray,* features the writings and words of Andrew Murray, one of the foremost devotional writers of the early twentieth century. Murray was a pastor in the Scottish Dutch Reformed church in South Africa. The fifty-two selections can be read daily, occasionally, or weekly. If you choose the latter option, you may wish to record somewhere else how well you achieved your spiritual goals that week.

However you decide to use this journal, it is my profound hope that you will not only have touched the heart of this great preacher and evangelist, but in your quiet moments alone, will have touched the heart of God.

This series is the first release of a forthcoming imprint entitled *LifeEssentials Books*. These books will concentrate on the priorities found at the intersection between faith and living. Based upon what we learn about God and His commands in Scripture, we will be able to better respond in all the critical areas of our lives by being renewed in His image in true holiness.

JAMES S. BELL JR.
Executive Editor
LifeEssentials Books

WAITING IS GOOD

1

The Lord is good to those who wait for Him, to the soul who seeks Him.
LAMENTATIONS 3:25

At our first entrance into the school of waiting upon God, the heart is chiefly set upon the blessings which we wait for. God graciously uses our need and desire for help to educate us for something higher than we were thinking of. We are seeking gifts; He, the Giver, longs to give Himself and to satisfy the soul with His goodness. It is just for this reason that He often withholds the gifts, and that the time of waiting is made so long. He is all the time seeking to win the heart of His child for Himself. He wishes that we should not only say, when He bestows the gift, How good is God! but that we should all the time be experiencing: *It is good* that a man should quietly wait; "The Lord *is good* to those who wait for Him."

What a blessed life the life of waiting then becomes, the continual worship of faith, adoring and trusting His goodness. As the soul learns its secret, every act or exercise of waiting just becomes a quiet entering into the goodness of God, to let it do its blessed work and satisfy our every need.

RESPONDING IN PRAYER

"Lord, the process of waiting is good because
You bestow Your own goodness upon us during this time.
Help me to worship and adore You for Yourself alone."

Continuing in prayer . . .

_____

_____

_____

_____

_____

_____

_____

_____

When in your life has God withheld the gift you sought but blessed you in a different way? How might that have been more beneficial?

_____

_____

_____

_____

_____

_____

_____

_____

_____

_____

_____

_____

SPIRITUAL GOALS FOR THE WEEK

_____

_____

_____

_____

_____

_____

_____

_____

WAITING FOR THE SOUL TO RIPEN

2

My soul, wait silently for God alone, for my expectation is from Him.
PSALM 62:5

$\mathcal{L}$ook up and see the great God upon His throne. He is Love—an unceasing and inexpressible desire to communicate His own goodness and blessedness to all His creatures. He longs and delights to bless. He has inconceivably glorious purposes concerning every one of His children, by the power of His Holy Spirit, to reveal in them His love and power. He waits with all the longings of a father's heart. He waits that He may be gracious unto you.

And each time you come to wait upon Him, or seek to maintain in daily life the holy habit of waiting, you may look up and see Him ready to meet you, waiting that He may be gracious unto you. Yes, connect every exercise, every breath of the life of waiting, with faith's vision of your God waiting for you.

And if you ask, "How is it, if He waits to be gracious, that even after I come and wait upon Him, He does not give the help I seek, but waits on longer and longer?" there is an . . . answer. The one is this: God is a wise husbandman who "waits for the precious fruit of the earth, waiting patiently for it" (James 5:7). He cannot gather the fruit till it is ripe. He knows when we are spiritually ready to receive the blessing to our profit and His glory. Waiting in the sunshine of His love is what will ripen the soul for His blessing.

RESPONDING IN PRAYER

"Lord, not only do I wait on You, but You also wait on me.
Give me a longing for You just as You long for my fellowship."

Continuing in prayer . . .

FOR REFLECTION

How much time do you spend in prayer, Bible study, and other disciplines simply asking and then allowing God to mature you, no matter how long it takes?

_____

_____

_____

_____

_____

_____

_____

_____

_____

_____

SPIRITUAL GOALS FOR THE WEEK

_____

_____

_____

_____

_____

_____

_____

HIS BODY AND BLOOD

| 3 |

And He took bread, gave thanks and broke it, and gave it to them, saying,
"This is My body which is given for you; do this in remembrance of Me."
Likewise He also took the cup after supper, saying,
"This cup is the new covenant in My blood, which is shed for you."

LUKE 22:19–20

*A*ll knowledge of the truth, and all acquaintance with the Gospel, are of no avail without the personal appropriation of that short phrase, *for me.* And that word of man has, on the other hand, its foundation in the word of Jesus, "For you."

So it was at the Lord's table. In speaking of His body and blood, the Savior addressed His disciples, and said to them: Given *for you;* shed *for you.*

How would the disciples in a later day feel themselves strengthened by that word! How could Peter in his deep fall, and Thomas in his grievous unbelief, and each of the others, fail to encourage themselves by remembering this: "He spoke to me so cordially, just as if it was meant for me alone, when He said, 'Given for you.'"

It is in this word that for me also the richest blessing of the Lord's Supper is wrapped up. For not less than to the first disciples does the Savior desire to say to everyone of His guests: "Given *for you.*" By His Holy Spirit, He is as near to us as to them; He can make us feel the power of His eye and His voice. Not only by reaching the bread to each one separately, but much more by the heavenly operation of His Holy Spirit, will Jesus address each one, saying, "Given for you."

RESPONDING IN PRAYER

"Lord, I thank You for the Lord's Supper which puts in tangible form
Your body broken for me and Your blood shed for me."

Continuing in prayer . . .

FOR REFLECTION

Ask God to give you a greater understanding and appreciation for the Lord's Supper. How would you describe its meaning in your own life?

_____

_____

_____

_____

_____

_____

_____

_____

_____

_____

_____

_____

SPIRITUAL GOALS FOR THE WEEK

_____

_____

_____

_____

_____

_____

_____

_____

_____

THROUGH CHRIST ALONE

| 4 |

For through Him we both have access by one Spirit to the Father.
EPHESIANS 2:18

*P*rayer is not merely coming to God to ask something from Him. It is above all fellowship with God, and being brought under the power of His holiness and love, till He takes possession of us, and stamps our entire nature with the lowliness of Christ, which is the secret of all true worship.

Yes, it is in Christ Jesus that we draw near to the Father, as those who have died with Christ and have entirely done with their own life, as those in whom He lives and whom He enables to say: "Christ lives in me." What we have said about the work that the Lord Jesus does in us to deliver us from prayerlessness, is true not only of the beginning of the life of prayer but all the day long. "Through Him" we have access to the Father. In this always, as in the whole spiritual life, Christ is all. "They saw no man save Jesus only."

May God strengthen us to a belief that there is certain victory prepared for us, and that the blessing will be what the heart of man has not conceived! God will do this for those who love Him.

RESPONDING IN PRAYER

"Lord, I wish to view prayer as a relationship in which I am transformed into Your likeness rather than Your granting me favors."

Continuing in prayer . . .

_____

_____

_____

_____

_____

_____

_____

_____

_____

What does the term "lowliness of Christ" mean to you in the context of how you relate to God and others?

_____

_____

_____

_____

_____

_____

_____

_____

_____

_____

_____

SPIRITUAL GOALS FOR THE WEEK

_____

_____

_____

_____

_____

_____

_____

_____

CONFORMED TO HIS IMAGE

5

But we are bound to give thanks to God always for you, brethren beloved
by the Lord, because God from the beginning chose you for salvation
through sanctification by the Spirit and belief in the truth.

2 THESSALONIANS 2:13

*O*ne of the most blessed expressions in regard to God's purpose concerning us in Christ is this word: "Predestined to be conformed to the image of His Son" (Romans 8:29). The man Christ Jesus is the elect of God; in Him election has its beginning and ending. "In Him we are chosen"; for the sake of our union with Him and to His glory our election took place. The believer who seeks in election merely the certainty of his own salvation, or relief from fear and doubt, knows very little of its real glory.

The purposes of election embrace all the riches that are prepared for us in Christ, and reach to every moment and every need of our lives. "Chosen in Him . . . that we should be holy and without blame before Him in love." It is only when the connection between election and sanctification is rightly apprehended in the church that the doctrine of election will bring its full blessing (2 Thessalonians 2:13; 1 Peter 1:2). It teaches the believer how it is God who must work all in him, and how he may rely even in the smallest matters upon the unchangeable purpose of God to work out itself in the accomplishment of everything that He expects of His people.

In this light, the word "Predestined to be conformed to the image of His Son" gives new strength to everyone who has begun to take *what Christ is* as the rule of *what he himself is to be.*

RESPONDING IN PRAYER

"Lord, it is comforting to know that You not only save us
but will make us holy and blameless in Your sight,
and that You have guaranteed that even before we were born."

Continuing in prayer . . .

What is your view of election—that God has elected, or chosen you to be His? Does it include the fact that you will be conformed to His Son through sanctification?

_____

_____

_____

_____

_____

_____

_____

_____

_____

_____

_____

SPIRITUAL GOALS FOR THE WEEK

_____

_____

_____

_____

_____

_____

_____

_____

ALL-SUFFICIENT GRACE

———— 6 ————

And He said to me, "My grace is sufficient for you, for My strength is made perfect in weakness." Therefore most gladly I will rather boast in my infirmities, that the power of Christ may rest upon me.

2 CORINTHIANS 12:9

*G*race is not only pardon of, but power over, sin; grace takes the place sin had in the life. Grace undertakes, as sin had reigned within in the power of death, to reign in the power of Christ's life. It is of this grace that Christ spoke, "My grace is sufficient for you." Paul answered, "I will rather boast in my infirmities . . . for when I am weak, then I am strong." When we are willing to confess ourselves utterly impotent and helpless, His grace comes in to work all in us, as Paul elsewhere teaches, "God is able to make *all grace* abound toward you; that you, *always* having *all sufficiency* in *all things,* have an abundance to *every good work.*"

Often a seeker after God and salvation has read his Bible long, and still has never seen the truth of a free and full and immediate justification by faith. When once his eyes were opened, and he accepted it, he was amazed to find it everywhere. Even many believers, who hold the doctrines of free grace as applied to pardon, have never seen its wondrous meaning. It undertakes to work our whole life in us, and *actually give us strength every moment* for whatever the Father would have us be and do. When God's light shines into our heart with this blessed truth, then we understand Paul's words, "Not I, but the grace of God." There again you have the twofold Christian life. The one, in which that "not I"—I am nothing, I can do nothing—has not yet become a reality. The other, when the wondrous exchange has been made and grace has taken the place of our effort.

RESPONDING IN PRAYER

"Lord, let me see Your grace as more than just pardon but extending to every area and every moment of my life, so that I may be sufficient for every good work."

Continuing in prayer . . .

_____

_____

_____

_____

How do you find the balance between letting God do the work in you and yet cooperating with your own effort?

_____

_____

_____

_____

_____

_____

_____

_____

_____

_____

_____

_____

SPIRITUAL GOALS FOR THE WEEK

_____

_____

_____

_____

_____

_____

_____

_____

_____

_____

PRAYING FOR THE LOST

------- 7 -------

"I tell you, no; but unless you repent you will all likewise perish."
LUKE 13:5

*I*f we are to learn to pray as we should, we must open eye and heart to the need around us.

We hear continually of the billions of heathen and Muslims living in midnight darkness, perishing for lack of the bread of life. We hear of millions of nominal Christians, the great majority of them almost as ignorant and indifferent as the heathen. We see millions in the Christian church, not ignorant or indifferent, and yet knowing little of a walk in the light of God or of the power of a life fed by bread from heaven. Each of us has his own circle—congregation, school, friends, mission—in which the great complaint is that the light and life of God are too little known. But if we believe what we profess, that God alone is able to help, that God certainly will help in answer to prayer, all this ought to make intercessors of us. It should motivate us to be people who give their lives to prayer for those around them.

Let us face and consider the need—each Christless soul going down into outer darkness, perishing of hunger, while there is bread enough and to spare! Millions each year die without the knowledge of Christ! Our own neighbors and friends, souls entrusted to us, die without hope! Christians around us live sickly, feeble, fruitless lives! Surely prayer is needed. Nothing—nothing but prayer to God for help will avail.

RESPONDING IN PRAYER

*"Lord, give me a broken heart for the lost who are perishing.
Sometimes it seems so overwhelming, but help me remember
that each prayer makes a difference to You."*

Continuing in prayer . . .

_____

_____

_____

_____

_____

FOR REFLECTION

Commit to praying more fervently for and sharing more passionately with your unsaved family, friends, and neighbors.

_____

_____

_____

_____

_____

_____

_____

_____

_____

_____

_____

SPIRITUAL GOALS FOR THE WEEK

_____

_____

_____

_____

_____

_____

_____

_____

GIVE UP EVERYTHING

| 8 |

"Again, the kingdom of heaven is like a merchant seeking beautiful pearls,
who, when he had found one pearl of great price,
went and sold all that he had and bought it."

MATTHEW 13:45–46

*T*he grace of God is very free. It is given without money and without price. And yet, on the other hand, Jesus said that every man who wants the pearl of great price must sacrifice his all, must sell all that he has to buy that pearl. It is not enough to see the beauty, the attractiveness and the glory, and almost to taste the gladness and the joy of this wonderful life as it has been set before you. You must become the possessor, the owner of the field. The man who found the field with a treasure, and the man who found the great pearl, were both glad; but they had not yet got it. They had found it, seen it, desired it, rejoiced in it; but they had not yet got it. Not until they went and sold all, gave up everything, and bought the ground, and bought the pearl.

Friends, there is a great deal that has to be given up: the world, its pleasures, its favor, its good opinion. You are to stand to the world in the same relation as Jesus did. The world rejected Him, and cast Him out, and you are to take up the position of your Lord, to whom you belong, and to follow with the rejected Christ. You have to give up everything.

RESPONDING IN PRAYER

"Lord, though I cannot earn Your grace, I must forsake all
that opposes You in order for Your grace to effectually
work in my life. I willingly commit to that now."

Continuing in prayer . . .

_____

_____

_____

_____

_____

_____

Ask God to show you anything that stands in the way of your receiving the pearl of great price. What are you not willing to "sell" in order to receive the favor of God?

_____

_____

_____

_____

_____

_____

_____

_____

_____

_____

_____

_____

SPIRITUAL GOALS FOR THE WEEK

_____

_____

_____

_____

_____

_____

_____

THE MARKS OF THE LAMB

Therefore, as the elect of God, holy and beloved, put on tender mercies,
kindness, humbleness of mind, meekness, longsuffering; bearing with one
another and forgiving one another, if anyone has a complaint against another;
even as Christ forgave you, so you also must do.

COLOSSIANS 3:12–13

The humble man feels no jealousy or envy. He can praise God when others are preferred and blessed before him. He can bear to hear others praised and himself forgotten, because in God's presence he has learned to say with Paul, "I am nothing." He has received the spirit of Jesus—who pleased not Himself and sought not His own honor—as the spirit of His life.

Amid what are considered the temptations to impatience and touchiness, to hard thoughts and sharp words, which come from the failings and sins of fellow Christians, the humble man carries the oft repeated injunction in his heart, and shows it in his life: "[Bear] with one another and [forgive] one another, if anyone has a complaint against another; even as Christ forgave you, so you also must do." He has learned that in putting on the Lord Jesus he has put on tender mercies, kindness, humbleness of mind, meekness, and longsuffering. Jesus has taken the place of self, and it is not an impossibility to forgive as Jesus forgave. His humility does not consist merely in thoughts or words of self-deprecation, but, as Paul puts it, in "a heart of humility," encompassed by compassion and kindness, humility and patience—the sweet and lowly gentleness recognized as the mark of the Lamb of God.

RESPONDING IN PRAYER

"Lord, my lack of humility causes me to have a difficult time
forgiving others. Help me not to seek my own recognition
but focus on lifting up others."

Continuing in prayer . . .

_____

_____

_____

_____

FOR REFLECTION

Have pride and lack of forgiveness been linked in your attitude toward someone who has hurt you in the past? Seek to reconcile with the person as soon as possible.

_____

_____

_____

_____

_____

_____

_____

_____

_____

_____

SPIRITUAL GOALS FOR THE WEEK

_____

_____

_____

_____

_____

_____

_____

CLOSE COMMUNION

———————— 10 ————————

*That which we have seen and heard we declare to you, that you also may
have fellowship with us; and truly our fellowship is with the Father
and with his Son, Jesus Christ.*

1 JOHN 1:3

*T*his is the fault of many who try to obey and try to believe; they do it in their
own strength, and they do not know that if the Lord Jesus is to reign in their
hearts, they must have close communion with Him every day. You cannot do all
He desires, but Jesus will do it for you. There are many Christians who fail here,
and on that account do not understand what it is to have fellowship with Jesus.

Do let me try and impress this upon you: God has given you a loving, living
Savior, and how can He bless if you do not meet Him?

The joy of friendship is found in intercourse; and Jesus asks for this every day,
that He may have time to influence me, to tell me of Himself, to teach me, to
breathe His Spirit unto me, to give me new life and joy and strength. And remember, intercourse with Jesus does not mean half-an-hour or an hour in your
closet. A man may study his Bible or his commentary carefully; he may look up
all the parallel passages in the chapter; when he comes out of his closet he may be
able to tell you all about it, and yet he has never met Jesus that morning at all. You
have prayed for five or ten minutes, and you have never met Jesus.

RESPONDING IN PRAYER

*"Lord, at times I may study Your Word and even pray
and yet come away never having truly met You.
Help me to commune deeply with You every day."*

Continuing in prayer . . .

_____

_____

_____

_____

_____

Look back to the times of deep fellowship with the Lord. What were the elements that made those times work and how can you enhance this experience?

_____

_____

_____

_____

_____

_____

_____

_____

_____

_____

_____

SPIRITUAL GOALS FOR THE WEEK

_____

_____

_____

_____

_____

_____

_____

_____

LOSING YOUR LIFE

By a new and living way which He consecrated for us,
through the veil, that is, His flesh.

HEBREWS 10:20

*E*very believer has "crucified the flesh with its passions and desires" (Galatians 5:
24). Every step on the new and living way for entering into God's holy presence
maintains the fellowship with the cross of Christ. The rent veil of the flesh has
reference, not only to Christ and His sufferings, but to our experience in the likeness of His sufferings.

Have we not here the reason why many Christians can never attain to close
fellowship with God? They have never yielded the flesh as an accursed thing to
the condemnation of the cross. They desire to enter into the holiest of all, and yet
allow the flesh with its desires and pleasures to rule over them. God grant that we
may rightly understand, in the power of the Holy Spirit, that Christ has called us
to hate our life, to lose our life, to be dead with Him to sin that we may live to
God with Him. There is no way to a full abiding fellowship with God, but
through the rent veil of the flesh, through a life with the flesh crucified in Christ
Jesus.

God be praised that the Holy Spirit ever dwells in us to keep the flesh in its
place of crucifixion and condemnation, and to give us the abiding victory over all
temptations.

RESPONDING IN PRAYER

"Lord, my fleshly nature wars against my spirit.
Grant me the grace to put to death the works of the flesh
and find victory in all my temptations."

Continuing in prayer . . . _____

_____

_____

_____

_____

_____

How do you have the proper balance of hating and losing your life and yet enjoying the earthly blessings God has given to you?

_____

_____

_____

_____

_____

_____

_____

_____

_____

_____

SPIRITUAL GOALS FOR THE WEEK

_____

_____

_____

_____

_____

_____

_____

_____

LIKE CHRIST

────────────┤12├────────────

"For the Father loves the Son, and shows Him all things
that He Himself does; and He will show Him
greater works than these, that you may marvel."
JOHN 5:20

*C*hild of God, it was not only for the only-begotten Son that a life plan was arranged, but for each of His children. In proportion to our dependence on the Father will this life plan be more or less perfectly worked out in our lives. The nearer the believer comes to this entire dependence of the Son—"He can do only what He sees His Father doing"—and then to His implicit obedience—"whatever the Father does the Son also does"—so much more will the promise be fulfilled to us: "For the Father loves the Son, and shows Him all things that He Himself does; and He will show Him greater works than these, that you may marvel." We are to be *like Christ*.

This dependence on the Father is first of all founded upon the faith that He will make His will known to us. Many do not believe that the Lord cares for them enough to daily teach them and to make known His will just as He did to Jesus. Believer, you are of more value to the Father than you realize. You are worth as much as the price He paid—that is, the blood of His Son. He therefore attaches the highest value to your smallest concerns and will guide even in what seems insignificant.

┌─────────────────────────────────────┐
│ RESPONDING IN PRAYER │
└─────────────────────────────────────┘

"Lord, it is hard to fathom the fact that You care so much
for me to daily teach me and make known Your will.
Help me to seek it and follow it."

Continuing in prayer . . . _____

_____

_____

_____

_____

_____

Do you really believe that God guides you in the most insignificant matters? Seek Him for even your smallest concerns.

_____

_____

_____

_____

_____

_____

_____

_____

_____

_____

SPIRITUAL GOALS FOR THE WEEK

_____

_____

_____

_____

_____

_____

_____

_____

NEARER TO GOD

Those who are Christ's have crucified the flesh with its passions and desires.
GALATIANS 5:24

$\mathcal{T}$he heaviest laden branches always bow the lowest. The greatest flow of water makes the deepest riverbed. The nearer the soul comes to God, the more His majestic presence makes it feel its littleness. It is this alone that makes it possible for each to count others better than himself. Jesus Christ, the holy One of God, is our example of humility. It is knowing that the Father had given all things into His hands, and that He was come from God and went to God, that He washed the disciples' feet that will make us humble. It is the divine presence, the consciousness of the divine life and the divine love in us, that will keep us humble.

It appears to many an impossibility to say: "I will not think self. I will esteem others better than myself." They ask grace to overcome the worst outbreaks of pride and vainglory, but an entire self-renunciation, such as Christ's, is too difficult and too high for them. If they only understood the deep truth: "He who humbles himself shall be exalted," "He who loses his life shall find it," they would not be satisfied with anything less than entire conformity to their Lord. And they would find that there is a way to overcome self and self-exaltation: to see it nailed to Christ's cross, and there keep it crucified continually through the Spirit (Galatians 5:24; Romans 8:13). Only he who heartily yields himself to live in the fellowship of Christ's death can grow to such humility.

RESPONDING IN PRAYER

*"Lord, let me be conscious of Your divine presence in a deeper way,
knowing that to be like You means dying to my sin nature
by identifying with Christ's death."*

Continuing in prayer . . .

_____

_____

_____

_____

_____

Study those passages in Paul's epistles that deal with our identity to Christ's death. Write out the full meaning of our being crucified with Christ and then participating in His life.

_____

_____

_____

_____

_____

_____

_____

_____

_____

_____

_____

SPIRITUAL GOALS FOR THE WEEK

_____

_____

_____

_____

_____

_____

_____

THE TREASURE WITHIN

"This is the covenant that I will make with the house of Israel: After those days, says the Lord, I will put My law in their minds, and write it on their hearts; and I will be their God, and they shall be My people."

JEREMIAH 31:33

In all our religion the great danger is giving more time and interest to the outward means than the inward reality. It is neither the intensity of your Bible study, nor the frequency or fervency of your prayers or good works that necessarily constitute a true spiritual life. We need to realize that as God is a Spirit so there is a spirit within us that can know and receive Him, become conformed to His likeness, and partake of the very dispositions that animate Him as God in His goodness and love.

Firmly settle this in your mind, that all our salvation consists in the manifestation of the nature, life, and spirit of Christ Jesus in our outward and inward new man. This alone renews and regains the first life of God in the soul of man.

Wherever you go, whatever you do, at home or abroad, do all with a desire for union with Christ, in imitation of His character and inclinations. Desire nothing so much as that which exercises and increases the spirit and life of Christ in your soul, and to have everything within you changed into the character and spirit of the holy Jesus.

Consider the treasure you have within you—the Savior of the world, the eternal Word of God, hidden in your heart as a seed of the divine nature—which is to overcome sin and death within you and generate the life of heaven in your soul.

RESPONDING IN PRAYER

"Lord, help me to more diligently study Your Word and hide Your promises in my heart in order to overcome sin and be more like Christ."

Continuing in prayer . . .

_____

_____

_____

_____

Set up a plan to broaden and deepen your study of God's Word in order to be able to live it and apply it in your life.

_____

_____

_____

_____

_____

_____

_____

_____

_____

_____

_____

SPIRITUAL GOALS FOR THE WEEK

_____

_____

_____

_____

_____

_____

_____

_____

_____

_____

_____

RICHES IN GLORY

That He would grant you, according to the riches of His glory, to be
strengthened with might through His Spirit in the inner man.
EPHESIANS 3:16

$\mathcal{L}$ook back to Ephesians 1:15–23 and its prayer on behalf of those who had already been sealed with the Spirit. Paul asked that God would give them the Spirit of wisdom and divine understanding that they might know the "exceeding greatness of His power" in all who believe. Oh, how believers need this great truth to secure a place in their hearts and thoroughly empower them! How believers who have received this need to be reminded of their calling to pray for those who have not received it. The health of the church as a whole, the spiritual strength of individual believers or churches, depends upon unceasing prayer in all perseverance and supplication for all the saints.

We must, also, study the prayer in 3:14–21 where Paul bows his knees and cries that God might grant something special "according to the riches of his glory." He desired that the believers might be strengthened with divine power so that they may be filled with all the fullness of God. Stop and meditate on this thought. True believers stand greatly in need of the prayers of all to whom the Spirit of supplication is given. The prayer is to be definite: pleading for the Spirit of divine power to fill their whole inner man, that Christ may dwell in their hearts, and they be rooted in love. All believers are to unite in prayer that God will bring into reality this strength for every believer.

RESPONDING IN PRAYER

"Lord, may Your divine power fill my entire inner being, that Christ
may dwell there in all His fullness, and that I may be rooted in love."

Continuing in prayer . . .

_____

_____

_____

_____

_____

FOR REFLECTION

How would you rate yourself in terms of "supplication for the saints" in your daily prayer life? Use this space to write prayers for those God has placed in your life.

_____

_____

_____

_____

_____

_____

_____

_____

_____

_____

_____

SPIRITUAL GOALS FOR THE WEEK

_____

_____

_____

_____

_____

_____

_____

VICTORIOUS FAITH

—| 16 |—

The Lord is your keeper; the Lord is your shade at your right hand.
PSALM 121:5

*Y*ou know that there are two ways to encounter and strive against sin. One is to endeavor to ward it off with all your might, seeking strength in the Word and in prayer. In this form of the conflict we use the power of the will. The other is to turn at the very moment of the temptation to the Lord Jesus in the silent exercise of faith and say to Him: "Lord, I have no strength. You are my keeper." This is the method of faith. "This is the victory that overcometh the world, even our faith" (1 John 5:4 KJV). Yes, this is indeed "the one thing needful," (Luke 10:42 KJV) because it is the only way in which Jesus, who is in Himself "The One Thing Needful," can maintain the work of His Spirit in us. It is by the exercise of faith without ceasing that the blessing will flow without ceasing.

Christ must be all to us every moment. It is of no avail to me that I have life on earth unless that life is renewed every moment by my inbreathing of fresh air. Even so must God actually renew, and uphold, and strengthen the divine life in me every moment. He does this for me in my union with Christ. Christ is the fullness of God, the life of God, the love of God prepared for us and communicating itself to us. The Spirit is the fullness of Christ, the life of Christ, the self-communicating love of Christ, surrounding us as the air surrounds the body.

RESPONDING IN PRAYER

"Lord, give me a vibrant, powerful faith that overcomes my problems and trials and takes advantage of the opportunities You bring my way."

Continuing in prayer . . .

_____

_____

_____

_____

_____

_____

FOR REFLECTION

If Jesus is "the one thing needful," write down all your needs to God and believe that He is the provider.

_____

_____

_____

_____

_____

_____

_____

_____

_____

_____

SPIRITUAL GOALS FOR THE WEEK

_____

_____

_____

_____

_____

_____

_____

GODLIKE LOVE

17

And we have known and believed the love that God has for us.
God is love, and he who abides in love abides in God, and God in him.
1 JOHN 4:16

*T*his is My commandment, that you love one another as I have loved you"
(John 15:12). The eternal life that works in us is the life of Jesus. It knows no other law than what we see in Him. It works with power in us what it worked
through Him. Jesus Himself lives in us and loves in and through us; we must believe in the power of this love in us, and in that faith love as He loved. Oh, do believe that this is true salvation—to love even as Jesus loves.

Brotherly love must be in deed and in truth. It is not mere feeling; faith
working by love is what has power in Christ. It manifests itself in all the characteristics that are enumerated in the Word of God. Contemplate its glorious image
in 1 Corinthians 13:4–7. Mark all the glorious encouragements to gentleness, to
longsuffering, to mercy. In all your conduct, let it be seen that the love of Christ
dwells in you. Let your love be a helpful, self-sacrificing love—like that of Jesus.
Hold all children of God, however frail and failing they may be, fervently dear.
Let love to them teach you to love all men. Let your household, and the church,
and the world see in you one with whom "love is greatest"; one in whom the
love of God has a full dwelling, a free working.

God is love. Jesus is the gift of this love, to bring love to you, to transplant you
into that life of Godlike love. Live in that faith and you shall not complain that you
have no power to love; the love of the Spirit shall be your power and your life.

RESPONDING IN PRAYER

*"Lord, give me a love that has all the qualities of Your own nature, so
that the world may clearly see the greatest love of all working within me."*

Continuing in prayer . . .

_____

_____

_____

_____

_____

How does your "household, and the church, and the world" see Christ's love manifested in you? What qualities listed above do you want in greater abundance?

_____

_____

_____

_____

_____

_____

_____

_____

_____

_____

_____

SPIRITUAL GOALS FOR THE WEEK

_____

_____

_____

_____

_____

_____

_____

_____

RESTING IN THE LORD

| 18 |

Rest in the Lord, and wait patiently for Him.

PSALM 37:7

*A*ll the exercises of the spiritual life—our reading and praying, our willing and doing—have their own great value. But they can go no further than this, that they point the way and prepare us in humility to look to and depend alone on God Himself, and in patience to wait for His time and mercy. The waiting is to teach us our absolute dependence on God's mighty working, and to make us in perfect patience place ourselves at His disposal. They that wait on the Lord shall inherit the land: the promised land and its blessing. The heirs must wait; they can afford to wait.

"Rest in the Lord, and wait patiently for Him." Scholars say that "rest in the Lord" may also be read, "Be silent to the Lord," or "Be still before the Lord." It is resting in the Lord, in His will, His promises, His faithfulness, and His love, that makes patience easy. And resting in Him is nothing but being silent to Him, still before Him. Having our thoughts and wishes, our fears and hopes, hushed into calm and quiet by that great "peace of God, which surpasses all understanding." That peace keeps the heart and mind when we are anxious for anything, because we have made our request known to Him.

The rest, the silence, the stillness, the patient waiting—all find their strength and joy in God Himself.

RESPONDING IN PRAYER

"Lord, please cause me to be silent before You more often so that I may contemplate Your glory, rest in Your life, and experience Your peace."

Continuing in prayer . . .

_____

_____

_____

_____

_____

Be silent before God in worship. After you have completed that exercise, write down your impressions of what you received from Him during that intimate fellowship.

_____

_____

_____

_____

_____

_____

_____

_____

_____

_____

_____

_____

SPIRITUAL GOALS FOR THE WEEK

_____

_____

_____

_____

_____

_____

_____

_____

THE JOY OF THE HOLY GHOST

───┤ 19 ├───

Whom having not seen you love. Though now you do not see Him,
yet believing, you rejoice with joy inexpressible and full of glory.
1 PETER 1:8

We all know what the power of joy is. There is nothing so attractive as joy; there is nothing that can help a man to bear and endure so much as joy. The Lord Jesus Himself "for the joy that was set before Him endured the cross." One is not living aright if he is living a sighing, trembling, doubting life. Come today and believe the joy of the Holy Ghost is meant for you. Does not the Scripture say, "Whom having not seen you love. Though now you do not see Him, yet believing, you rejoice with joy inexpressible and full of glory"? Do you not believe that this blessed, adorable, inconceivably beautiful Son of God, the delight of the Father, could fill your heart with delight day and night if He were always present? And do you not believe that He loves you more than a bridegroom loves his bride? Do you not believe that, having bought you with His blood, Jesus is longing for you? He needs you to satisfy His heart of love.

Begin to believe with your whole heart, "The joy of the Holy Ghost is my portion, for the Holy Ghost secures to me without interruption the presence and the love of Jesus."

RESPONDING IN PRAYER

"Lord, fill me with that inexpressible joy that comes from knowing that You love us more than a bridegroom, having bought us with Your own life."

Continuing in prayer . . .

Jesus is longing to give you joy right now. From the previous reading, how can you better experience the joy He offers?

_____

_____

_____

_____

_____

_____

_____

_____

_____

_____

_____

SPIRITUAL GOALS FOR THE WEEK

_____

_____

_____

_____

_____

_____

_____

_____

UNITY IN THE TRINITY

20

"That they all may be one, as You, Father, are in Me, and I in You;
that they also may be one in Us, that the world may believe that You sent me."
JOHN 17:21

*T*he mystery of the Holy Trinity is the mystery of the Christian life, the mystery of holiness. The three are one, and we need to enter ever more deeply into the truth that none of the three ever works separately or independently of the others. The Son reveals the Father, and the Father reveals the Son. The Father gives not Himself, but the Spirit; the Spirit speaks not of Himself, but cries "Abba, Father!" The Son is our sanctification, our life, our all: the fullness is in Him. And yet we must always bow our knees to the Father for Him to reveal Christ in us, for Him to establish us in Christ. The Father does not do this without the Spirit; we have to ask to be strengthened mightily by the Spirit that Christ may dwell in us. Christ gives the Spirit to those who believe and love and obey; the Spirit again gives Christ, formed within and dwelling in the heart.

So in each act of worship, each step of growth, each blessed experience of grace, all three persons are actively engaged. The one is ever three, the three are ever one.

To apply this in the life of holiness, faith in the Holy Trinity must be a living, practical reality. In every prayer to the Father to sanctify you, take up your position in Christ, and do it in the power of the Spirit within you. In every exercise of faith in Christ as your sanctification, let your posture be that of prayer to the Father and trust in Him as He delights to honor the Son, and of quiet expectancy of the Spirit's working, through whom the Father glorifies the Son.

RESPONDING IN PRAYER

"Lord, may I better understand the purposes of each member of the
Holy Trinity and deepen my relationship with all three. I pray that
Father, Son, and Holy Spirit all work in my life to the fullest."

Continuing in prayer . . .

_____

_____

_____

_____

Name three characteristics of each member of the Trinity that you appreciate or have had a direct effect on your life. Explain the impact.

_____

_____

_____

_____

_____

_____

_____

_____

_____

_____

_____

_____

_____

SPIRITUAL GOALS FOR THE WEEK

_____

_____

_____

_____

_____

_____

_____

_____

_____

_____

OBEDIENCE AS SACRIFICE

———— 21 ————

Though He was a Son, yet He learned obedience
by the things which He suffered.
HEBREWS 5:8

*H*ave we indeed given to obedience the supreme place of authority over us that God means it to have, as the inspiration of every action and of every approach to Him? If we yield ourselves to the searching of God's Spirit, we may find that we never gave obedience the importance it deserves in our scheme of life, and that this is the cause of all our failure in prayer and in work. The deeper blessings of God's grace, and the full enjoyment of God's love and nearness, have been beyond our reach, simply because obedience was never made what God would have it be—the starting point and the goal of our Christian life.

May God arouse in us an earnest desire to know His will fully concerning this truth. Let us pray that the Holy Spirit may show us how far short the Christian's life falls where obedience does not rule all. May He help us see how that life can be exchanged for one of full surrender to absolute obedience, and how sure it is that God in Christ will enable us to live it out. As the disobedience of Adam in paradise closed its gate, and the obedience of the Second Adam opened it, obedience in us leads us in the new and living way to God's heart, and opens the way for God to come and dwell in our hearts.

May God make obedience—since it is the one sacrifice He asks of us—the one sacrifice we offer Him.

RESPONDING IN PRAYER

"Lord, I want to see obedience become both my motivation
and my goal. Let me follow the example of my humble Savior,
who through His obedience led us into the presence of the Father."

Continuing in prayer . . .

_____

_____

_____

_____

_____

FOR REFLECTION

List areas of your own life in which you have found it difficult to obey God.
Then seek Him to discover how you can know the joy of greater obedience.

_____

_____

_____

_____

_____

_____

_____

_____

_____

_____

_____

_____

SPIRITUAL GOALS FOR THE WEEK

_____

_____

_____

_____

_____

_____

_____

_____

_____

SEASONS OF PRAYER

$$\overline{\boxed{22}}$$

Praying always with all prayer and supplication in the Spirit, being watchful to this end with all perseverance and supplication for all the saints.

EPHESIANS 6:18

*P*aul felt so deeply the unity of the body of Christ, and he was so sure that that unity could only be realized in the exercise of love and prayer, that he pleaded with the believers at Ephesus unceasingly and fervently to pray for all saints, not only in their immediate circle, but in all the Church of Christ of whom they might hear. Unity is strength. As we exercise this power of intercession with all perseverance, we shall be delivered from self with all its feeble prayers, and lifted up to that enlargement of heart in which the love of Christ can flow freely and fully through us.

The great lack in true believers often is that in prayer they are occupied with themselves, and with what God must do for them. Let us realize that we have here a call to every believer to give himself without ceasing to the exercise of love and prayer. It is as we forget ourselves, in the faith that God will take charge of us, and yield ourselves to the great and blessed work of calling down the blessing of God on our brethren, that the whole church will be fitted to do its work in making Christ known to every creature. This alone is the healthy and the blessed life of a child of God who has yielded himself wholly to Christ Jesus.

Pray for God's children and the church around you. Pray for all the work in which they are engaged, or ought to be. Pray at all seasons in the Spirit for all God's saints. There is no blessedness greater than that of abiding communion with God.

RESPONDING IN PRAYER

"Lord, help me to focus on the needs of my immediate family, community, nation, and the world at large. Help me to remember that my prayers can bring change on a global scale through the church."

Continuing in prayer . . .

_____

_____

_____

_____

What percentage of your prayers are caught up in yourself in comparison to the needs of others? How can you increase your prayers for others?

_____

_____

_____

_____

_____

_____

_____

_____

_____

_____

_____

SPIRITUAL GOALS FOR THE WEEK

_____

_____

_____

_____

_____

_____

_____

_____

WHAT GOD WILLS

—————| 23 |—————

"Father, if it is Your will, remove this cup from Me;
nevertheless not My will, but Yours, be done."
LUKE 22:42

*Y*ou find men trying to change their own hearts, to change their own wills, to change their inclinations, but they have found that they could not change it. But God changes it. I have read the story of a Christian woman losing her temper week after week, and going to her bedroom and praying and crying to God for deliverance, and telling how she did it for years and no deliverance came. The will was right; it has been so with many. That was evidence that God's work was in them, that they did not sit down with the thought, "Well, never mind, there is no great harm." But they never get rest in it. Their will was set upon doing the will of God, though they utterly failed in performing it.

Therefore I say to you, my fellow Christians, though you have not attained yet to the doing of God's will, begin and hold fast that and say, "I will what God wills." Say that. In affliction say—even though your heart trembles and you cannot submit; though you cannot bring your heart to do what you want and to be perfectly submissive—say, "Lord, I will what You will. I give up my will and I choose Your will, though my heart refuses to rest." Or, with regard to any sin that is troubling you and conquering you, say it to God, "Lord, I will to do what Thou hast commanded."

RESPONDING IN PRAYER

"Lord, I have tried so often to change my behavior
in compliance with Your will but continue to fail.
I will to do what You will and surrender to Your grace."

Continuing in prayer . . .

_____

_____

_____

_____

_____

FOR REFLECTION

Sometimes we really don't want to give up our secret sins and unconsciously program ourselves to fail. Ask God to search your soul for areas where you in fact resist His will. List below any He reveals to you.

_____

_____

_____

_____

_____

_____

_____

_____

_____

_____

_____

SPIRITUAL GOALS FOR THE WEEK

_____

_____

_____

_____

_____

_____

_____

_____

YIELDING COMPLETELY

24

It is written: "Be holy, for I am holy."
1 PETER 1:16

Then, since all these things will be dissolved, what manner of persons ought you to be in holy conduct and godliness." Brethren, the time is short! The world is passing away. The heathen are perishing. Christians are sleeping. Satan is active and mighty. God's holy ones are the hope of the church and the world. It is they their Lord can use. Shall we not seek to be such as the Father commands, holy, as He is holy? Shall we not yield ourselves afresh and undividedly to Him who is our sanctification, and to His Blessed Spirit, to make us holy in all behaviors and pieties?

Oh! Shall we not, in thought of the love of our Lord Jesus, in thought of the coming glory, in view of the coming end, of the need of the Church and the world, give ourselves to be holy as He is holy? Then we may have power to bless each believer we meet with the message of what God will do, and in concert with them we may be a light and a blessing to this perishing world.

RESPONDING IN PRAYER

"Lord, help me unite with other believers to let this weak church become a powerhouse of Your grace and light in a dying world. Sanctify me so that others may be drawn to You."

Continuing in prayer . . .

_____

_____

_____

_____

_____

_____

_____

_____

How does your church activity, your fellowship with other believers, allow you to give a stronger witness to the world? Make a plan to deepen your church experience.

_____

_____

_____

_____

_____

_____

_____

_____

_____

_____

_____

_____

SPIRITUAL GOALS FOR THE WEEK

_____

_____

_____

_____

_____

_____

_____

_____

HAPPINESS NEEDS HOLINESS

25

*You love righteousness and hate wickedness; therefore God, Your God,
has anointed You with the oil of gladness more than Your companions.*
PSALM 45:7

*H*oliness is essential to true happiness; happiness is essential to true holiness. If you would have joy, the fullness of joy, an abiding joy which nothing can take away, be holy as God is holy. Holiness is blessedness. Nothing can darken or interrupt our joy but sin. Whatever be our trial or temptation, the joy of Jesus, in which, Peter says, "you now rejoice with joy inexpressible," can more than compensate and outweigh. If we lose our joy, it must be sin. It may be an actual transgression, or an unconscious following of self or the world; it may be the stain on conscience of something doubtful, or it may be unbelief that would live by sight, and thinks more of itself and its joy than of the Lord alone: Whatever it be, nothing can take away our joy but sin.

If we would live lives of joy, assuring God and man and ourselves that our Lord is everything, is more than all to us, oh, let us be holy! Let us glory in Him who is our holiness. In His presence "is fullness of joy" (Psalm 16:11). Let us live in the kingdom which is joy in the Holy Ghost.

The Spirit of holiness is the Spirit of joy, because He is the Spirit of God. It is the saints, God's holy ones, who will shout for joy.

And happiness is essential to true holiness. If you would be a holy Christian, you must be a happy Christian. Jesus was anointed by God with 'the oil of gladness,' that He might give us 'the oil of joy.' In all our efforts after holiness the wheels will move heavily if there be not the oil of joy; this alone removes all strain and friction, and makes the onward progress easy and delightful.

RESPONDING IN PRAYER

*"Lord, often I seek to be happy without being holy.
Help me to realize the close relationship between the two
and the need to begin with Your command to be holy."*

Continuing in prayer . . .

_____

_____

_____

Why are you sometimes frustrated in your attempts to be happy? When has walking with God in holiness produced unexpected happiness?

_____

_____

_____

_____

_____

_____

_____

_____

_____

_____

_____

SPIRITUAL GOALS FOR THE WEEK

_____

_____

_____

_____

_____

_____

_____

_____

_____

THE DIVINE TEACHER

─────┤26├─────

And do not be conformed to this world, but be transformed
by the renewing of your mind, that you may prove what is
that good and acceptable and perfect will of God.
ROMANS 12:2

*B*eliever, it is not enough that the light of Christ shines on you in the Word,
the light of the Spirit must shine in you. Each time you come to the Word in
study, in hearing a sermon, or reading a religious book, there ought to be, as dis-
tinct as your intercourse with the external means, a definite act of self-abnegation,
denying your own wisdom, and yielding yourself in faith to the Divine Teacher.
Believe very distinctly that He dwells within you. He seeks the mastery, the sanctification of your inner life, in entire surrender and obedience to Jesus.

Rejoice to renew your surrender to Him. Reject the spirit of the world
which is still in you, with its wisdom and self-confidence; come, in poverty of
spirit, to be led by the Spirit that is of God. "Do not be conformed to this world,
but be transformed by the renewing of your mind, that you may prove what is
that good and acceptable and perfect will of God."

It is a transformed, renewed life, which only wants to know God's perfect
will, that will be taught by the Spirit. Cease from your own wisdom; wait for the
wisdom in the inward parts which God has promised.

RESPONDING IN PRAYER

"Lord, I renounce my own wisdom and self-confidence and seek to be
taught by Your Spirit to know and do Your good and perfect will."

Continuing in prayer . . .

_____

_____

_____

_____

_____

_____

The Book of Proverbs speaks of our essential need for divine wisdom to be able to do God's will. Write down those areas in your life where you need special wisdom.

_____
_____
_____
_____
_____
_____
_____
_____
_____
_____
_____

SPIRITUAL GOALS FOR THE WEEK

_____
_____
_____
_____
_____
_____
_____

SUBJECTION TO CHRIST

—— 27 ——

As many as are led by the Spirit of God, these are sons of God.
ROMANS 8:14

*F*rom Scripture we learn how the flesh has its twofold action: From the flesh springs not only unrighteousness, but self-righteousness. Both must be confessed and surrendered to Him whom the Spirit would reveal and enthrone as Lord, our Mighty Savior. All that is carnal and sinful, all the works of the flesh, must be given up and cast out. But no less must all that is carnal, however religious it appears—all confidence in the flesh, all self-effort and self-struggling—be rooted out. The soul, with its power, must be brought into the captivity and subjection of Jesus Christ. In deep and daily dependence on God must the Holy Spirit be accepted, waited for, and followed.

Thus walking in faith and obedience, we may count on the Holy Spirit to do a divine and most blessed work within us. "If we live by the Spirit"—this is the faith that is needed. And then, if we believe that God's Spirit dwells in us, by the Spirit let us live; this is the obedience that is asked. In the faith of that Holy Spirit who is in us, we know that we have sufficient strength to walk by the Spirit, and yield ourselves to His mighty working, to work in us to will and to do all that is pleasing in God's sight.

RESPONDING IN PRAYER

"Lord, help me to understand what are the works of my own flesh,
even when self-effort and struggling appear to be good.
Bring all of my being into subjection to Christ."

Continuing in prayer . . .

_____

_____

_____

_____

_____

_____

FOR REFLECTION

In what areas does your own self-effort or self-confidence take the place of relying completely on God's Spirit? Examine yourself and ask God to show those areas; write the results below.

_____

_____

_____

_____

_____

_____

_____

_____

_____

_____

SPIRITUAL GOALS FOR THE WEEK

_____

_____

_____

_____

_____

_____

_____

_____

FROM CURSE TO BLESSING

28

Having wiped out the handwriting of requirements
that was against us, which was contrary to us.
And He has taken it out of the way, having nailed it to the cross.
COLOSSIANS 2:14

*O*n the cross the Son of God enters into the fullest union with man—enters into the fullest experience of what it was to have become a son of man, a member of a race under the curse. It is in death that the prince of life conquers the power of death; it is in death alone that He can make me partaker of that victory. The life He imparts is a life from the dead; each new experience of the power of that life depends upon the fellowship of the death.

The death and the life are inseparable. All the grace which Jesus the Saving One gives is given only in the path of fellowship with Jesus the Crucified One. Christ came and took my place; I must put myself in His place, and abide there. And there is but one place which is both His and mine—that place is the Cross. His in virtue of His free choice; mine by reason of the curse of sin. He came there to seek me; there alone I can find Him. When He found me there, it was the place of cursing; this He experienced, for "cursed is everyone who hangs on a tree" (Galatians 3:13). He made it a place of blessing; this I experience, for Christ hath delivered us from the curse, being made a curse for us.

RESPONDING IN PRAYER

"Lord, I am in awe when I think of Your taking the curse for
my own sins. Help me to experience the full blessings of
deliverance and more fully praise and worship You."

Continuing in prayer . . .

_____

_____

_____

_____

_____

_____

What individual "curses" have turned into blessings in your own life because of
God's mercies bestowed on you at Calvary?

_____

_____

_____

_____

_____

_____

_____

_____

_____

_____

_____

_____

SPIRITUAL GOALS FOR THE WEEK

_____

_____

_____

_____

_____

_____

_____

_____

A PRIESTLY HEART

29

But you are a chosen generation, a royal priesthood, a holy nation,
His own special people, that you may proclaim the praises of Him
who called you out of darkness into His marvelous light.

1 PETER 2:9

*O*ne of the chief reasons for the feeble life in the church is the mistaken idea that man's happiness is the main object of God's grace. A fatal error! God's aim is far holier and far higher. He saves men on purpose that they in turn shall carry out His purpose in saving their fellow men. Each believer is appointed to be the means of imparting to others the new life he has received.

Those who are saved have the holy calling of being channels of God's grace to others. The feeble state of the church is largely due to the fact that most Christians imagine that their chief concern is to desire and receive sufficient grace to reach heaven after death. The church must so proclaim the Gospel that each saved soul shall apprehend its message, "Saved to serve," "Saved to save others." "You . . . are a royal priesthood."

A royal priesthood! The priestly heart is above all things a sympathetic heart, in which the love of Christ constrains us to win souls for Him. And that by virtue of two compelling motives: love to Christ, whom I shall please and honor in winning others to love Him; and love for souls, which will constrain me to sacrifice everything that others may share this heavenly life.

A priestly heart! A heart that has access to God in prayer and intercession for those who are yet unconverted. A priestly heart that, having pleaded in prayer for souls, has courage to speak to them of Christ.

RESPONDING IN PRAYER

"Lord, I hope to realize more each day that my true happiness comes not directly but indirectly by being a channel of Your grace to others. Help me be a mediator for others."

Continuing in prayer . . .

_____

_____

_____

_____

Do you have a priestly heart? How can you better intercede for others and gain a new compassion for their hurts?

_____

_____

_____

_____

_____

_____

_____

_____

_____

_____

SPIRITUAL GOALS FOR THE WEEK

_____

_____

_____

_____

_____

_____

_____

_____

JOYFUL BRANCHES

30

*"These things I have spoken to you, that My joy
may remain in you, and that your joy may be full."*

JOHN 15:11

*T*o many Christians the thought of a life wholly abiding in Christ is one of strain and painful effort. They cannot see that the strain and effort only come as long as we do not yield ourselves unreservedly to the life of Christ in us. The very first words of the parable are not yet opened up to them: "I am the true vine; I undertake all and provide for all; I ask nothing of the branch but that it yields wholly to Me and allows Me to do all. I engage to make and keep the branch all that it ought to be." Ought it not to be an infinite and unceasing joy to have the vine thus work all? Each moment let us allow the blessed Son of God in His love to maintain our life.

"That My joy may remain in you." We are to have Christ's own joy in us. And what is Christ's own joy? There is no joy like love. There is no joy but love. Christ had just spoken of the Father's love and His own abiding in it and of His having loved us with that same love. His joy is nothing but the joy of love, of being loved and of loving. It was the joy of receiving His Father's love and abiding in it and then the joy of passing on that love and pouring it out on sinners.

It is this joy He wants us to share: The joy of being loved of the Father and of Him; the joy of in our turn loving and living for those around us. This is just the joy of being truly branches: abiding in His love and then giving up ourselves in love to bear fruit for others.

RESPONDING IN PRAYER

"Lord, I am so grateful that the abiding process is not one of painful effort, but rather of surrender. Help me to experience the joy of Your love and give it to those around me."

Continuing in prayer . . .

_____

_____

_____

_____

Ask God to reveal to you how better to abide in Him without strain. How can you yield rather than strive to bear your own fruit?

_____

_____

_____

_____

_____

_____

_____

_____

_____

_____

SPIRITUAL GOALS FOR THE WEEK

_____

_____

_____

_____

_____

_____

_____

_____

THE MASTER'S PLANS

31

"No longer do I call you servants, for a servant does not know what
his master is doing; but I have called you friends, for all things that
I heard from My Father I have made known to you."

JOHN 15:15

It is a blessed thing to be Christ's servant; His redeemed ones delight to call themselves His slaves. Christ had often spoken of the disciples as His servants. In His great love, our Lord now says, "No longer do I call you servants." With the coming of the Holy Spirit, a new era was to be inaugurated. "A servant does not know what his master is doing." The servant has to obey without being consulted or admitted into the secret of all his master's plans. "But I have called you friends, for all things that I have heard from My Father I have made known unto you."

Christ's friends share with Him in all the secrets the Father has entrusted to Him.

Let us think what this means. When Christ spoke of keeping His Father's commandments, He did not mean merely what was written in Holy Scripture but those special commandments that were communicated to Him day by day and from hour to hour. It was of these He said, "The Father loves the Son, and shows Him all things that He Himself does; and He will show him greater works than these" (John 5:20). All that Christ did was God's working. God showed it to Christ, so that He carried out the Father's will and purpose, not as man often does, blindly and unintelligently, but with full understanding and approval.

RESPONDING IN PRAYER

"Lord, what an incredible privilege it is to be called Your friend.
I pray for greater intimacy with You and understanding of
Your ways so that I will be a good friend to You."

Continuing in prayer . . .

_____

_____

_____

_____

_____

Would you describe your relationship with the Lord for the most part as one of servant or friend? Based on today's reading, what can you do to better understand His plans?

_____

_____

_____

_____

_____

_____

_____

_____

_____

_____

_____

SPIRITUAL GOALS FOR THE WEEK

_____

_____

_____

_____

_____

_____

_____

A DIVINE WARNING

"You say, 'I am rich, have become wealthy, and have need of nothing'—
and do not know that you are wretched, miserable, poor, blind, and naked."
REVELATION 3:17

The secret spirit of [the church of] Laodicea—we are rich and increased in goods, and have need of nothing—may prevail where it is not suspected. The divine warning—poor and wretched and miserable—finds little response just where it is most needed. Revelation 3:17 is a very searching Scripture.

Let us not rest content with the thought that we are taking an equal share with others in the work that is being done, or that men are satisfied with our efforts in Christ's service, or even point to us as examples. Let our only desire be to know whether we are bearing all the fruit Christ is willing to give through us as living branches, in close and living union with Himself. We need to determine whether we are satisfying the loving heart of the great husbandman, our Father in heaven, in His desire for more fruit.

The Word comes with divine authority to search and test our life; the true disciple will heartily surrender himself to its holy light and will earnestly ask that God Himself may show what may be lacking in the measure or the character of the fruit he bears. Let us believe that the Word is meant to lead us on to a fuller experience of the Father's purpose of love, of Christ's fullness, and of the wonderful privilege of bearing much fruit in the salvation of men.

RESPONDING IN PRAYER

"Lord, in my complacency I sometimes feel satisfied when I am
actually poor and wretched spiritually. I pray that You will open
my eyes to see my needs but be encouraged that You can meet them."

Continuing in prayer . . .

_____

_____

_____

_____

_____

Review the words *wretched, miserable, poor, blind,* and *naked* and ask God to fill in opposites that you can become in Him.

_____

_____

_____

_____

_____

_____

_____

_____

_____

_____

_____

SPIRITUAL GOALS FOR THE WEEK

_____

_____

_____

_____

_____

_____

_____

DIVINE RESCUE

| 33 |

"O wretched man that I am! Who will deliver me from this body of death?"
ROMANS 7:24

*B*lessed be God when a man learns to say: "What a wretched man I am!" from the depth of his heart. He is on the way to the eighth chapter of Romans.

There are many who make this confession a pillow for sin. They say that Paul had to confess his weakness and helplessness in this way; who are they that they should try to do better? So the call to holiness is quietly set aside. Would God that every one of us has learned to say these words in the very spirit in which they are written here! When we hear sin spoken of as the abominable thing that God hates, do not many of us wince before the Word? Would that all Christians who go on sinning and sinning would take this verse to heart. If ever you utter a sharp word, say, "What a wretched man I am!" And every time you lose your temper, kneel down and understand that it was never meant by God that this was to be the state in which His child should remain.

Instead, we are to take this word into our daily life and say it every time we are touched about our own honor, and every time we say sharp things, and every time we sin against the Lord God and against His self-sacrifice. Forget everything else and cry out. "What a wretched man I am! Who will rescue me from this body of death?"

Why should you say this whenever you commit sin? Because it is when a man is brought to this confession that deliverance is at hand.

RESPONDING IN PRAYER

"Lord, whenever I sin help me to see its utter sinfulness
and confess that only You can release me from my body of death.
I desire Your deliverance over and over again."

Continuing in prayer . . .

_____

_____

_____

_____

Why is it humbling and frustrating to continue to ask for forgiveness and admit our helplessness and depravity repeatedly? Why is it necessary?

_____

_____

_____

_____

_____

_____

_____

_____

_____

_____

_____

SPIRITUAL GOALS FOR THE WEEK

_____

_____

_____

_____

_____

_____

_____

_____

_____

THE OMNIPOTENCE OF GOD

──────── 34 ────────

I was with you in weakness, in fear, and in much trembling.
1 CORINTHIANS 2:3

The whole of Christianity is a work of God's omnipotence. Look at the birth of Christ Jesus. That was a miracle of divine power, and it was said to Mary: 'With God nothing will be impossible.' It was the omnipotence of God. Look at Christ's resurrection. We are taught that is was according to the exceeding greatness of His mighty power that God raised Christ from the dead.

Every tree must grow on the root from which it springs. An oak tree three hundred years old grows all the time on the one root from which it had its beginning. Christianity had its beginning in the omnipotence of God, and in every soul it must have its continuance in that omnipotence. All the possibilities of the higher Christian life have their origin in a new apprehension of Christ's power to work all God's will in us.

I want to call upon you now to come and worship an almighty God. Have you learned to deal so closely with an almighty God that you know omnipotence is working in you? In outward appearance there is often little sign of it. The apostle Paul said: "I was with you in weakness, in fear, and in much trembling. And . . . my preaching [was] . . . in demonstration of the Spirit and of power." From the human side there was feebleness, from the divine side there was divine omnipotence. And that is true of every godly life.

RESPONDING IN PRAYER

"Lord, let me remember that Your strength is demonstrated in my weakness, and in all things help me to depend on You and Your power to work Your will in my life."

Continuing in prayer . . .

_____

_____

_____

_____

_____

Name a time when you felt that you simply could not accomplish some task and because of that God made it a resounding success.

_____

_____

_____

_____

_____

_____

_____

_____

_____

_____

_____

SPIRITUAL GOALS FOR THE WEEK

_____

_____

_____

_____

_____

_____

_____

_____

RESTORING JOY

| 35 |

Restore to me the joy of your salvation,
and uphold me with Your generous Spirit.
PSALM 51:12

*W*hen a believer has fallen into a low, sad state of feeling, he often tries to lift himself out of it by chastening himself with dark and doleful fears. Such is not the way to rise from the dust, but to continue in it. . . . It is not the law, but the Gospel which saves the seeking soul at first; and it is not a legal bondage, but Gospel liberty which can restore the fainting believer afterwards. Slavish fear brings not back the backslider to God, but the sweet wooings of love allure him to Jesus' bosom.

Are you this morning thirsting for the living God, and unhappy because you cannot find him to the delight of your heart? Have you lost the joy of religion, and is this your prayer, "Restore to me the joy of your salvation"? Are you conscious also that you are barren, like the dry ground; that you are not bringing forth the fruit unto God which He has a right to expect of you; that you are not so useful in the church, or in the world, as your heart desires to be? Then here is exactly the promise which you need, "I will pour water upon him that is thirsty." You shall receive the grace you so much require, and you shall have it to the utmost reach of your needs.

RESPONDING IN PRAYER

"Lord, I have had my emotional lows at times and my fears of Your
displeasure have alienated me from You. Draw me back to You
by the sweetness of Your love so that I may not be condemned."

Continuing in prayer . . .

_____

_____

_____

_____

_____

When your commitment to God cools, how might you overcome the obstacles that stand in your way? What initiates this process that should be avoided?

_____

_____

_____

_____

_____

_____

_____

_____

_____

_____

_____

_____

SPIRITUAL GOALS FOR THE WEEK

_____

_____

_____

_____

_____

_____

_____

_____

DUTY OVER PRIVILEGE

───────┤ 36 ├───────

"You are My friends if you do whatever I command you."
JOHN 15:14

*A*s we obey the commands, we shall know the love more fully. Christ had already said: "If you keep My commandments, you will abide in My love." He counts it needful to repeat the truth again: the one proof of our faith in His love, the one way to abide in it, the one mark of being true branches is to do the things He commands us.

He began with absolute surrender of His life for us. He can ask nothing less from us. This alone is a life in His friendship.

This truth of the imperative necessity of obedience, doing all that Christ commands us, has not the place in our Christian teaching and living that Christ meant it to have. We have given a far higher place to privilege than to duty. We have not considered implicit obedience as a condition of true discipleship. The secret thought that it is impossible to do the things He commands us, and that therefore it cannot be expected of us, and a subtle and unconscious feeling that sinning is a necessity have frequently robbed both precepts and promises of their power. The whole relation to Christ has become clouded and lowered, the waiting on His teaching, the power to hear and obey His voice, and through obedience to enjoy His love and friendship, have been enfeebled by the terrible mistake.

Do let us try to return to the true position, take Christ's words as most literally true, and make nothing less of the law of our life: "You are my friends if you do whatever I command you." Surely our Lord asks nothing less than that we heartily and truthfully say, "Yea, Lord, what You command, that will I do."

RESPONDING IN PRAYER

"Lord, help me to do exactly what You command in Scripture promptly and wholeheartedly. I want to know the full meaning of Your commands, so please help me understand Scripture better."

Continuing in prayer . . .

_____

_____

_____

FOR REFLECTION

As you study the Bible, do you wait on God to reveal its truth and then pray for the power to obey Him, and thus enjoy closer fellowship?

_____

_____

_____

_____

_____

_____

_____

_____

_____

_____

_____

SPIRITUAL GOALS FOR THE WEEK

_____

_____

_____

_____

_____

_____

_____

_____

THE GREATEST FATHER

37

He said to them, "When you pray, say:
'Our Father in heaven, hallowed be your name. Your kingdom come.'"
LUKE 11:2

Just think what a book could be written of all the memories that there have been on earth of wise and loving fathers. Just think of what this world owes to the fathers who have made their children strong and happy in giving their lives to seek the welfare of their fellowmen. And then think how all this is but a shadow —a shadow of exquisite beauty, but still a shadow of what the Father in heaven is to His children on earth.

What a gift Christ bestowed on us when He gave us the right to say: "Father!" "The Father of Christ," "Our Father," "My Father."

And then, "Our Father in heaven," our heavenly Father. We count it a great privilege as we bow in worship to know that the Father comes near to us where we are upon earth. But we soon begin to feel the need of rising up to enter into His Holy presence in heaven, to breathe its atmosphere, to drink in its spirit, and to become truly heavenly minded. And as we in the power of thought and imagination leave earth behind, and in the power of the Holy Spirit enter the holiest of all, where the seraphs worship, the word "heavenly Father" gets a new meaning, and our hearts come under an influence that can abide all the day.

And as we then gather up our thoughts of what fatherhood on earth has meant, and hear the voice of Christ saying, "How much more"—we feel the distance there is between the earthly picture and the heavenly reality, and can only bow in lowly, loving adoration, "Father, our Father, my Father."

RESPONDING IN PRAYER

"Lord, when I look at examples of earthly fathers who have greatly loved and cared for their children, I realize that they pale in comparison to Your perfect fatherhood. Help me to receive Your father love and be a better child."

Continuing in prayer . . .

_____

_____

_____

_____

FOR REFLECTION

What impact has your earthly father had on your perceptions of your heavenly father? If any of his flaws have gotten in the way, ask God to enlighten your mind and heart.

_____

_____

_____

_____

_____

_____

_____

_____

_____

_____

_____

_____

SPIRITUAL GOALS FOR THE WEEK

_____

_____

_____

_____

_____

_____

_____

_____

THE SPIRIT'S OPERATION

---38---

That you may have a walk worthy of the Lord, fully pleasing Him,
being fruitful in every good work and increasing in the knowledge of God.
COLOSSIANS 1:10

*T*here is in the Vine such fullness, the care of the divine husbandman is so sure of success, that the much fruit is not a demand but the simple promise of what must come to the branch that lives in the double abiding—he in Christ, and Christ in him. The same "bears much fruit" (John 15:5). It is certain.

Have you ever noticed the difference in the Christian life between work and fruit? A machine can do work; only life can bear more fruit. A law can compel work; only love can spontaneously bring forth fruit. Work implies effort and labor; the essential idea of fruit is that it is the silent, natural, restful produce of our inner life. The gardener may labor to give his apple tree the digging and manuring, the watering, and the pruning it needs. He can do nothing to produce the apple; the tree bears its own fruit. So in the Christian life: "The fruit of the Spirit is love, joy, peace." The healthy life bears much fruit.

The connection between work and fruit is perhaps best seen in the expression "being fruitful in every good work" (Colossians 1:10). It is only when good works come as the fruit of the indwelling Spirit that they are acceptable to God. Under the compulsion of law and conscience, or the influence of inclination and zeal, men may be most diligent in good works, and yet find that they have but little spiritual result. There can be no reason but this—their works are man's effort, instead of being the fruit of the Spirit the restful, natural outcome of the Spirit's operation within us.

RESPONDING IN PRAYER

"Lord, I want to allow You to be the gardener in my life to
do all the pruning and cultivating, weeding and fertilizing,
necessary for me to bear healthy and abundant fruit."

Continuing in prayer . . . _____

_____

_____

_____

FOR REFLECTION

When have you done something that you considered to be very effective in serving God's kingdom, only to find that it didn't really work out well? How might you link this result to working through your own strength?

_____

_____

_____

_____

_____

_____

_____

_____

_____

_____

_____

SPIRITUAL GOALS FOR THE WEEK

_____

_____

_____

_____

_____

_____

_____

_____

THE TREASURES OF HEAVEN

"If you abide in Me, and My words abide in you,
you will ask what you desire, and it shall be done for you."
JOHN 15:7

*C*hrist was sending out His disciples, and they were ready to give their life for the world; to them He gave the disposal of the treasures of heaven. Their prayers would bring the Spirit and the power they needed for their work.

Let us realize that we can only fulfill our calling to bear much fruit by praying much. In Christ are hid all the treasures men around us need; in Him all God's children are blessed with all spiritual blessings; He is full of grace and truth. But it needs prayer, much prayer, strong believing prayer, to bring those blessings down. And let us equally remember that we cannot appropriate the promise without a life given up for men. Many try to take the promise and then look round for what they can ask. This is not the way; but the very opposite. Get the heart burdened with the need of souls and the command to save them, and the power will come to claim the promise.

Let us claim it as one of the revelations of our wonderful life in the Vine: He tells us that if we ask in His name, in virtue of our union with Him, whatsoever it be, it will be done to us. Souls are perishing because there is too little prayer. God's children are feeble because there is so little prayer. The faith of this promise would make us strong to pray; let us not rest till it has entered into our very heart and drawn us in the power of Christ to continue and labor and strive in prayer until the blessing comes in power.

RESPONDING IN PRAYER

"Lord, so often I think of the things I want for myself
rather than the eternal destiny of others. Help me to labor
in prayer for all the things that matter to You first."

Continuing in prayer . . .

_____

_____

_____

_____

FOR REFLECTION

What has been your most successful prayer "adventure" and what methods made it work so well? How might this happen with issues you face today?

_____

_____

_____

_____

_____

_____

_____

_____

_____

_____

_____

_____

SPIRITUAL GOALS FOR THE WEEK

_____

_____

_____

_____

_____

_____

_____

_____

HIS GOOD PURPOSE

—————————————— 40 ——————————————

For it is God who works in you both to will and to do for His good pleasure.
PHILIPPIANS 2:13

I am sure there is many a heart that says, "Ah, but that absolute surrender implies so much!" Someone says: "Oh, I have passed through so much trial and suffering, and there is so much of the self-life still remaining, and I dare not face the entire giving of it up, because I know it will cause so much trouble and agony."

Alas! Alas! That God's children have such thoughts of Him, such cruel thoughts. Oh, I come to you with a message, fearful and anxious one.

God does not ask you to give the perfect surrender in your strength or by the power of your will; God is willing to work it in you. Do we not read, "For it is God who works in you both to will and to do for His good pleasure"? And that is what we should seek for—to go on our faces before God, until our hearts learn to believe that the everlasting God Himself will come in to turn out what is wrong, to conquer what is evil, and to work what is well-pleasing in His blessed sight. God Himself will work it in you.

Look at the men in the Old Testament, like Abraham. Do you think it was by accident that God found that man, the father of the faithful and the friend of God, and that it was Abraham himself, apart from God, who had such faith and such obedience and such devotion? You know it is not so. God raised him up and prepared him as an instrument for His glory.

Did not God say to Pharaoh, "For this cause have I raised thee up, for to show in thee my power?" And if God said that of him, will not God say it far more of every child of His?

RESPONDING IN PRAYER

*"Lord, help me not to focus on the negative aspects of surrender
but realize that the work is Yours and You will do
great things in my life if I trust in Your ways."*

Continuing in prayer . . .

_____

_____

_____

_____

FOR REFLECTION

Ask God to be the one to raise you up and be an instrument of His glory. In what areas of your walk with Him would you like to see this happen?

_____

_____

_____

_____

_____

_____

_____

_____

_____

_____

_____

SPIRITUAL GOALS FOR THE WEEK

_____

_____

_____

_____

_____

_____

_____

_____

_____

THE GREATEST DECISION

| 41 |

Casting down arguments and every high thing that exalts itself against the knowledge of God, bringing every thought into captivity to the obedience of Christ.

2 CORINTHIANS 10:5

*W*hen the call is heard to come and now begin anew a true life of obedience, there are many who desire to do so, and try quietly to slip into it. They think that by more prayer and Bible study they will grow into it—it will gradually come. They are greatly mistaken. The word God uses in Jeremiah might teach them their mistake. "Turn, O backsliding children, turn to Me." A soul that is in full earnest and has taken the vow of full obedience may grow out of feeble obedience into a fuller one. But there is no growing out of disobedience into obedience. A turning back, a turning away, a decision, a crisis, is needed. And that comes only by the very definite insight into what has been wrong, and the confession of that with shame and penitence. Then alone will the soul seek for that divine and mighty cleansing from all its filthiness which prepares for the consciousness of the gift of the new heart, and God's Spirit in it, causing us to walk in His statutes.

If you would hope to lead different lives, to become possessors of a Christlike obedience unto death, begin by beseeching God for the Holy Spirit of conviction, to show you all your disobedience and to lead you in humble confession to the cleansing God has provided. Rest not till you have received it.

RESPONDING IN PRAYER

"Lord, cleanse me of all unrighteousness and help me make the decision to turn from my disobedience completely. Show me where I am wrong and help me to fully repent."

Continuing in prayer . . .

_____

_____

_____

_____

_____

At what point in your life did a marked turning away, decision, or crisis, lead you to break with disobedience? What situation now might cause a similar experience?

_____
_____
_____
_____
_____
_____
_____
_____
_____
_____
_____
_____

SPIRITUAL GOALS FOR THE WEEK

_____
_____
_____
_____
_____
_____
_____
_____

UNCHANGING HOLINESS

42

"Therefore you shall be perfect, just as your Father in heaven is perfect."
MATTHEW 5:48

"There is none holy [but] the Lord" (1 Samuel 2:2); there is no holiness but what He has, or rather what He is and gives. The quality is not something we do or attain: it is the communication of the divine life, the inbreathing of the divine nature, the power of the divine presence resting on us. And our power to become holy is to be found in the call of God: the Holy One calls us to Himself that He may make us holy in possessing Himself. He not only says "I am holy," but "I am the Lord, who makes holy." Because the call comes from the God of infinite power and love, we may have the confidence: We can be holy.

The call no less reveals the standard of holiness. "Like the Holy One who called you, be yourselves also holy." There is not one standard for God and another for man. The nature of light is the same, whether we see it in the sun or in a candle; the nature of holiness remains unchanged, whether it be God or man in whom it dwells. The Lord Jesus could say nothing less than, "You shall be perfect just as your Father in heaven is perfect." When God calls us to holiness, He calls us to Himself and His own life. The more carefully we listen to the voice, and let it sink into our hearts, the more will all human standards fall away and only the words be heard, "Holy as I am holy."

RESPONDING IN PRAYER

"Lord, though Your standard of holiness is daunting, it is a comfort to know that You are able to put me on the path to perfection—not only to know Your commands but to do them."

Continuing in prayer . . .

_____

_____

_____

_____

_____

Describe what holiness in your own life should look like. How can your life better mirror God's character?

_____

_____

_____

_____

_____

_____

_____

_____

_____

_____

_____

SPIRITUAL GOALS FOR THE WEEK

_____

_____

_____

_____

_____

_____

_____

_____

BOTH DEATH AND LIFE

---| 43 |---

Likewise you also, reckon yourselves to be dead indeed to sin,
but alive to God in Christ Jesus our Lord.

ROMANS 6:11

If we want to have the real Christ that God has given us, the real Christ that died for us, in the power of His death and resurrection, we must take our stand here. But many Christians do not understand what the sixth chapter of the epistle to the Romans teaches us. They do not know that they are dead to sin. They do not know it, and therefore Paul instructs them, "Do you not know that as many of us as were baptized into Christ Jesus were baptized into His death?"

"How can we who are dead to sin in Christ live any longer therein?" We have indeed the death and life of Christ working within us. But, alas, most Christians do not know this, and therefore do not experience or practice it. They need to be taught that their first need is to be brought to the recognition, to the knowledge, of what has taken place in Christ on Calvary, and what has taken place in their becoming united to Christ. The man must begin to say, even before he understands it, "In Christ I am dead to sin." It is a command: "Reckon yourselves dead to sin." Get hold of your union to Christ; believe in the new nature within you, that spiritual life which you have from Christ, a life that has died has been raised again.

RESPONDING IN PRAYER

"Lord, give me the wisdom to comprehend how death and life work
in me at the same time. Help me to continue to put to death
the deeds of the body, so that I may be alive in the Spirit."

Continuing in prayer . . . _____

_____

_____

_____

_____

_____

Write down some scriptural examples of why you are dead to sin and commit them to memory.

_____

_____

_____

_____

_____

_____

_____

_____

_____

_____

_____

_____

_____

SPIRITUAL GOALS FOR THE WEEK

_____

_____

_____

_____

_____

_____

_____

_____

THE SECRET OF WAITING

—— |44| ——

Wait on the Lord; be of good courage, and He shall strengthen your heart.
PSALM 27:14

*W*e are seeking gifts; He, the giver, longs to give Himself and to satisfy the soul with His goodness. It is exactly for this reason that He often withholds the gifts, and that the time of waiting is made so long.

What a blessed life the life of waiting then becomes—the continual worship of faith, adoring and trusting His goodness. As your soul learns this secret, every act or exercise of waiting simply becomes a quiet entering into the goodness of God, to let it do its blessed work and satisfy all our needs. And every experience of God's goodness gives the work of waiting new attractiveness. Instead of taking refuge only in time of need, there comes a great longing to wait continually and all day long. And however our duties and daily responsibilities occupy our time and minds, our souls get more familiar with the secret art of always waiting.

Waiting becomes the habit and constant attitude, the second nature and breath of your soul.

RESPONDING IN PRAYER

"Lord, at times I wait when I want specific answers to prayer,
but help me to wait as a continual spiritual discipline.
Even in the midst of busyness, may my soul wait upon You."

Continuing in prayer . . . _____

_____

_____

_____

_____

_____

_____

_____

How would you explain from today's reading how your soul can wait upon God while your mind and body are busy with the day's activities?

_____

_____

_____

_____

_____

_____

_____

_____

_____

_____

_____

SPIRITUAL GOALS FOR THE WEEK

_____

_____

_____

_____

_____

_____

_____

_____

_____

_____

TIME IN PRAYER

45

Pray without ceasing.
1 THESSALONIANS 5:17

In prayer the most essential element is faith. The whole of salvation, the whole of the new life, is by faith and therefore also by prayer. There is far too much prayer that brings nothing, because there is little faith in it. Before I pray, and while I pray, and after I have prayed, I must ask: Do I pray in faith? I must say, I believe with my whole heart.

To arrive at this faith, we must take time in prayer—time to set ourselves silently and trustfully before God and to be refreshed in His presence; time to have our soul sanctified in fellowship with God; time for the Holy Spirit to teach us to hold fast and use trustfully the word of promise. We do not gain earthly knowledge, possessions, food, or fellowship with friends without it taking time. We should not expect to learn how to pray, how to enjoy the power and the blessedness of prayer, if we do not take time with God.

And then there must be not only time every day but perseverance from day to day. Time is required to grow in the certainty that we are acceptable to the Father and that our prayer has power, in the confidence which knows that our prayer is according to His will and is heard. Prayer is conversation and fellowship with God in which God has time and opportunity to work in us; in which our souls die to their own will and power and become bound up and united with God.

RESPONDING IN PRAYER

*"Lord, I dedicate so much time to other activities,
even spiritual ones, but I find concentrated prayer so difficult.
Help me to give You the time to work in me."*

Continuing in prayer . . .

_____

_____

_____

_____

Ask God if you are spending enough time in prayer each day and how much time you should set aside from now on. Come up with a plan to do it.

_____

_____

_____

_____

_____

_____

_____

_____

_____

_____

_____

SPIRITUAL GOALS FOR THE WEEK

_____

_____

_____

_____

_____

_____

_____

_____

PURIFIED VESSELS

46

Though the fig tree may not blossom, nor fruit be on the vines; though the labor of the olive may fail, and the fields yield no food; though the flock be cut off from the fold, and there be no herd in the stalls—yet I will rejoice in the Lord, I will be joyful in the God of my salvation.

HABAKKUK 3:17–18

*E*ven in its highest revelations in Christians that have made the greatest progress, faith rests not on what is to be seen of the work of God or on the experiences of it, but on the work of God as spiritual, invisible, . . . and inconceivable. If you have gone into this time of discouragement and desire to return to the true life according to the promise, my counsel is to not be surprised if it comes to you slowly or if it appears to be involved in darkness. If you know that you have given yourself to God wholeheartedly, and if you know that God, really and with His whole heart, waits to fulfill His promise in you with divine power, then rest in silence before His face and hold fast your integrity.

Although the cold of winter appears to bury everything in death, say with the prophet Habakkuk: "Though the fig tree may not blossom nor fruit be on the vines . . . yet I will rejoice in the Lord, I will be joyful in the God of my salvation" (3:17–18). Do this, and you will know God, and God will know you. If you have set yourself before God as an empty, purified vessel, to become full of His Spirit, then continue to regard yourself so and keep silence before Him. If you have believed that God has received you to fill you as a purified vessel—purified through Jesus Christ and by your entire surrender to Him—then abide in this attitude day by day, and you may depend upon it that the blessing will grow and begin to flow.

RESPONDING IN PRAYER

"Lord, no matter what I encounter in the way of want or discouragement, help me to continue to rejoice and trust in You, knowing that in Your timing I will become a full, pure vessel."

Continuing in prayer . . .

FOR REFLECTION

Ask God to give you the perspective to rejoice in some of the difficult trials you have recently or presently experienced.

_____

_____

_____

_____

_____

_____

_____

_____

_____

_____

SPIRITUAL GOALS FOR THE WEEK

_____

_____

_____

_____

_____

_____

_____

_____

FORSAKING FALSEHOOD

---47---

Therefore, putting aside lying, each one speak truth with his neighbor,
for we are members of one another.

EPHESIANS 4:25

*T*he believer who desires to live unceasingly in the consciousness that he has been sealed with the Holy Spirit will find in his faith the assurance that the power and presence of that Spirit within him makes it possible to live without grieving Him.

And yet the danger is so near and so strong. Unless we live entirely under the power of the Spirit, we may not hear the warning. It is essential to make a study of all the possible hindrances to His work in us. The context (from verse 25) speaks of falsehood, anger, stealing, corrupt speech, and transgressions of the law of love. These were to be put far away; everything that is against God's law must grieve the Holy Spirit.

But there is more. Think of all the commands of the Lord Jesus as expressed through the Beatitudes concerning being poor in spirit, meek, merciful, and pure in heart; through all His teaching concerning bearing our cross, denying self, forsaking the world and following Him; down to His last commands to His disciples to love one another as He had loved them and to serve one another. These are some of the distinctive marks of the heavenly life Christ came to bring. Everything that is not in harmony with these must grieve the Spirit and prevent the enjoyment of His presence.

RESPONDING IN PRAYER

"Lord, I do not wish to grieve the Holy Spirit by allowing falsehood
of any kind in my life, so please shine the light of truth on all
my dealings with others—that my actions may be based on love."

Continuing in prayer . . .

_____

_____

_____

_____

Search your heart to see if there be any false dealing with your neighbor or a family member. If there is, ask God to help you make amends and deal fairly from now on.

_____

_____

_____

_____

_____

_____

_____

_____

_____

_____

_____

SPIRITUAL GOALS FOR THE WEEK

_____

_____

_____

_____

_____

_____

_____

_____

HEARING AND DOING

───────┤48├───────

But be doers of the word, and not hearers only, deceiving yourselves.
JAMES 1:22

In life, in science and art, in business, the only way of truly knowing is doing. What a man cannot do he does not thoroughly know. The only way to know God, to taste His blessedness, is through the doing of His will. That proves whether it is a God of my own sentiment and imagination that I confess, or the true and living God who rules all. Only by doing His will can I prove I love and accept it, and make myself one with it. And there is no possible way under heaven of being united to God but by being united to His will through doing it.

The self-delusion of hearing and not doing is conquered in the quiet of the inner chamber, in the spirit in which I do my private Bible reading, in the determination to absolutely settle the issue of, "I am going to do whatever God says."

Here is how we should approach a portion of God's Word. Suppose it to be the Sermon on the Mount. I begin with the first Beatitude: "Blessed are the poor in spirit," I ask, "What does this mean? Am I obeying this injunction? Am I earnestly seeking, day by day, to maintain this disposition? Am I willing to wait, and plead with Christ, and believe that He can develop it in me? Am I going to *do* this—to be poor in spirit? Or shall I again be a hearer and not a doer?"

RESPONDING IN PRAYER

"Lord, help me to settle, each day, the question of whether I am going to do exactly what You say. Help me not to block out Your voice or refuse to obey You. I seek to put Your Word into practice."

Continuing in prayer . . .

_____

_____

_____

_____

_____

At times do you commit to putting into practice what you understand in the Word and then forget its teaching? How can you overcome this weakness?

_____

_____

_____

_____

_____

_____

_____

_____

_____

_____

_____

SPIRITUAL GOALS FOR THE WEEK

_____

_____

_____

_____

_____

_____

_____

FORGIVING LOVE

*"But if you do not forgive, neither will
your Father in heaven forgive your trespasses."*
MARK 11:26

We must learn that as forgiveness of our sins was one of the first things Jesus did for us, forgiveness of others is one of the first that we can do for Him. To the new heart there is a joy even sweeter than that of being forgiven—the forgiving of others. The joy of being forgiven is only that of a sinner and of earth. The joy of forgiving is Christ's own joy, the joy of heaven. Oh, come and see that it is nothing less than the work that Christ Himself does, and the joy with which He Himself is satisfied that you are called to participate in.

Here you can bless the world. It is as the forgiving One that Jesus conquers His enemies and binds His friends to Himself. It is as the forgiving One that Jesus has set up His kingdom and continually extends it. It is through the same forgiving love, not only preached but *shown in the life of His disciples,* that the church will convince the world of God's love. If the world sees men and women loving and forgiving as Jesus did, it will be compelled to confess that God is truly with them.

And if it still seems too hard and too high, remember that this is only a reflection from the natural heart. It has no taste for this joy and can never attain it. But in union with Christ we can do it: He who abides in Him walks even as He walked. If you have surrendered yourself to follow Christ in everything, then He will by His Spirit enable you to do this too.

RESPONDING IN PRAYER

"Lord, reveal to me the power of forgiveness so that the world can see what You have done and know the same joy of freedom from their sins."

Continuing in prayer . . .

_____

_____

_____

_____

_____

When has your act of forgiveness displayed God's love to someone in a very tangible way? When has your lack of forgiveness blocked the flow of His love?

_____

_____

_____

_____

_____

_____

_____

_____

_____

_____

_____

SPIRITUAL GOALS FOR THE WEEK

_____

_____

_____

_____

_____

_____

_____

_____

NEW COVENANT LIFE

—— 50 ——

Are you so foolish? Having begun in the Spirit,
are you now being made perfect by the flesh?

GALATIANS 3:3

*T*he proof that our religion is very much that of the religious flesh is that the sinful flesh will be found to flourish along with it. It was thus with the Galatians. While they were making a fair show in the flesh, and glorying in it, their daily life was full of bitterness and envy and hatred, and other sins. They were biting and devouring one another. Religious flesh and sinful flesh are one; no wonder that, with a great deal of religion, temper and selfishness and worldliness are so often found side by side. The religion of the flesh cannot conquer sin.

What a contrast to the religion of the New Covenant! What is the place the flesh has there? "Those who are Christ's have crucified the flesh with its passions and desires" (Galatians 5:24). Scripture speaks of the will of the flesh, the mind of the flesh, the lust of the flesh. All this the true believer has seen to be condemned and crucified in Christ; he has given it over to the death. He not only accepts the Cross, with its bearing of the curse, and its redemption from it, as his entrance into life; he glories in it as his only power day by day to overcome the flesh and the world. "I am crucified with Christ."

"God forbid that I should glory except in the cross of our Lord Jesus Christ, by which the world has been crucified to me." Even as nothing less than the death of Christ was needed to inaugurate the New Covenant, and the resurrection life that animates it, there is no entrance into the true New Covenant life other than by a partaking of that death.

RESPONDING IN PRAYER

"Lord, it is hard for me to comprehend that 'religious flesh' is
just as much a failure as 'sinful flesh' as we try to please You.
Grant me Your resurrection life, which is the only true way."

Continuing in prayer . . .

_____

_____

_____

_____

In what practical ways can you glory in the cross in your own life? How do you bear the cross and have others noticed its positive effects?

_____

_____

_____

_____

_____

_____

_____

_____

_____

_____

_____

SPIRITUAL GOALS FOR THE WEEK

_____

_____

_____

_____

_____

_____

_____

_____

_____

GLAD TIDINGS

---51---

Now hope does not disappoint, because the love of God has been poured out in our hearts by the Holy Spirit who was given to us.
ROMANS 5:5

In Jesus it was the Spirit that led Him to the work of love for which He was anointed, to preach glad tidings to the poor and deliverance to the captives; through that same Spirit He offered Himself a sacrifice for us. The Spirit comes to us freighted with all the love of God and of Jesus: The Spirit is the Love of God.

And when that Spirit enters us, His first work is, God has "poured out [His love] in our hearts by the Holy Spirit who was given to us" (Romans 5:5). What He gives is not only the faith or the experience of how greatly God loves, but something infinitely more glorious. The love of God, as a spiritual existence, as a Living Power, enters our hearts. It cannot be otherwise, for the love of God exists in the Spirit; the outpouring of the Spirit is the inpouring of love.

This love now possesses the heart. That one same love with which God loves Jesus, and ourselves, and all His children, and which overflows to all the world, is within us, and is, if we know it, and trust it, and give up to it, the power for us to live in too. The Spirit is the life of the love of God; the Spirit in us is the love of God taking up abode within us.

RESPONDING IN PRAYER

"Lord, pour Your love into my heart by the Holy Spirit that I may better share the good news of this love with those You have brought into my life. May it possess them as it does me."

Continuing in prayer . . .

_____

_____

_____

_____

_____

Is there a difference between the way you describe the love of God to others and the way you demonstrate it? How can you bring these two closer together?

_____

_____

_____

_____

_____

_____

_____

_____

_____

_____

_____

SPIRITUAL GOALS FOR THE WEEK

_____

_____

_____

_____

_____

_____

_____

HIS HOLY PRESENCE

────────── 52 ──────────

And it came to pass, as He was praying in a certain place,
when He ceased, that one of His disciples said to Him,
"Lord, teach us to pray, as John also taught his disciples."

LUKE 11:1

*D*o I know what prayer is? Do I know what it is to meet the great God? Do I know how to take hold of God and hold Him fast? Do I know how to take hold of His strength? Do I know what the full fellowship and communion of God is? Begin to sit still until you realize His holy presence, and feel how little you are fit to speak to Him.

Lord, I know not how to pray. I may know many things to pray for but not what I need most. My prayer may be right—"Lord, deliver me from pride and self-will"—and yet I may not know how sadly I need pride to be removed. Perhaps God wants me to be delivered from pride and I pray for that; and yet I have never seen myself as God sees me, and I have never been truly convicted of my pride. So you can pray for other things and never come to the real point of what you need.

You need before everything in prayer a deep consciousness of your ignorance. What a wonderful blessing if I come into this ignorance. The Holy Spirit will be my helper in prayer. This blessed ignorance is one of the most remarkable elements of faith. Abraham went out not knowing whither he went. It was a beautiful ignorance, it taught him to trust God.

┌─────────────────────────────────────┐
│   RESPONDING IN PRAYER   │
└─────────────────────────────────────┘

"Lord, help me not to be afraid of ignorance but to see
it as a stepping stone to really be taught by You.
Show me what I truly need and deal with my pride."

Continuing in prayer . . .

_____

_____

_____

_____

FOR REFLECTION

Pride is so intrinsic to the fallen nature that many of us cannot recognize much of it. Ask God to help you see your pride and forsake it by His grace.

_____

_____

_____

_____

_____

_____

_____

_____

_____

_____

SPIRITUAL GOALS FOR THE WEEK

_____

_____

_____

_____

_____

_____

_____

JAMES S. BELL, JR. serves as acquisitions manager at Moody Press and has received cover credit for more than fifteen books that he compiled, edited, or introduced. His specialty is classic literature, inclusing revisions of *Quo Vadis* and *Ben Hur*. He lives in West Chicago with his wife, Margaret, and children: Rosheen, Brendan, Brigit, and Caitlin.